MR. POPPER'S PENGUINS

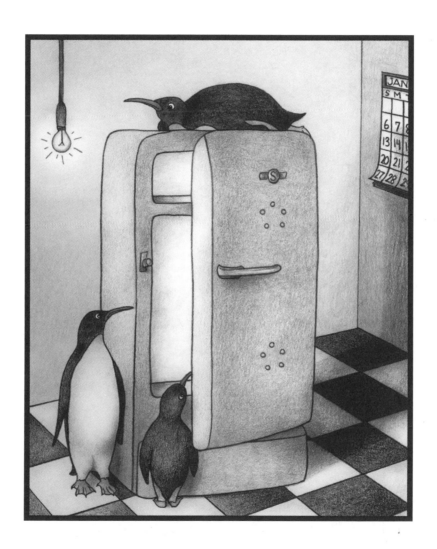

Student Study Guide

Leigh Lowe & Jessica Watson

MEMORIA PRESS
www.MemoriaPress.com

MR. POPPER'S PENGUINS

STUDENT STUDY GUIDE
Leigh Lowe & Jessica Watson
Cover Illustration by Starr Steinbach

ISBN 978-1-61538-841-7

Second Edition © 2017 Memoria Press

Cover illustration by Starr Steinbach

Contents

Teaching Guidelines..4

Chapter 1: Stillwater 6

Chapter 2: The Voice in the Air............................8

Chapter 3: Out of the Antarctic 10

Chapter 4: Captain Cook 12

Chapter 5: Troubles with a Penguin 14

Chapter 6: More Troubles...................................16

Chapter 7: Captain Cook Builds A Nest............18

Chapter 8: Penguin's Promenade 20

Chapter 9: In the Barber Shop...........................24

Chapter 10: Shadows 26

Chapter 11: Greta 28

Chapter 12: More Mouths to Feed....................30

Chapter 13: Money Worries................................32

Chapter 14: Mr. Greenabuam............................34

Chapter 15: Popper's Performing Penguins......38

Chapter 16: On the Road 40

Chapter 17: Fame..42

Chapter 18: April Winds......................................44

Chapter 19: Admiral Drake 46

Chapter 20: Farewell, Mr. Popper......................48

PREPARING TO READ:

REVIEW
- Orally review any previous vocabulary.
- Review the plot of the book as read so far.
- Periodically review the concepts of character, setting, and plot.

STUDY GUIDE PREVIEW
- Reading Notes:
  - Read aloud together.
  - This section gives the student key characters, places, and terms that are relevant to a particular time period, etc.
- Vocabulary:
  - Read aloud together so that students will recognize words when they come across them in their reading.
- Comprehension Questions:
  - Read through these questions with students to encourage purposeful reading.

READING:
- Student reads the chapter (or selection of the chapter for that lesson) independently or to the teacher (for younger students).
- For younger students, you can alternate between teacher-read and student-read passages. Model good reading skills. Encourage students to read expressively and smoothly. The teacher may occasionally take oral reading grades.
- While reading, mark each vocabulary word as you come across it.
- Have students take note in their study guide margin of pages where a Comprehension Question is answered.

AFTER READING:

VOCABULARY

- Look at each word within the context that it is used, and help your student come up with the best synonym that defines the word. (Make sure it is a synonym the student knows the meaning of.)
- Record the word's meaning in the students' study guides. (Use students' knowledge of Latin and other vocabulary to decipher meanings.)

COMPREHENSION QUESTIONS

- Older students can answer these questions independently, but younger students (2nd-4th) need to answer the questions orally, form a good sentence, and then write it down, using correct punctuation, capitalization, and spelling. (You may want to write the sentence down for the younger student after forming it orally, and then let the student copy it perfectly.)
- It is not necessary to write the answer to every question. Some may be better answered orally.
- Answering questions and composing answers is a valuable learning activity. Questions require students to think; writing a concise answer is a good composition exercise.

QUOTATIONS AND DISCUSSION QUESTIONS

- Use the Quotations and Discussion Questions section of each lesson as a guide to your oral discussion of the key concepts in the chapter that may not be covered in the Comprehension Questions.
- These talking points can take your oral discussion to a higher level than covered in the students' written work. Use this time as an opportunity to introduce higher-level thinking. You can introduce concepts the students may not be mature enough to fully understand yet, but that would be beneficial for them to begin thinking about.
- A key to the Discussion Questions is in the back of the Teacher Guide.

ENRICHMENT

- The Enrichment activities include composition, copywork, sequencing, research, mapping, drawing, literary terms, and more.
- This section has a variety of activities in it, but the most valuable activity is composition. Your student should complete at least one composition assignment. Proof the student's work and have the student copy composition until grammatically perfect. Insist on clear, concise writing. For younger students, start with 2-3 sentences, and do the assignment together. The student can form good sentences orally as you write them down, and then the student copies them.
- These activities can be completed as time and interest allow. Do not feel you need to complete all of these activities. Choose the ones that you feel are the best use of your students' time.

QUIZZES AND TEST

- There are two quizzes, one for the first half of the book, one for the second.
- A final comprehensive exam is also included. This exam covers the material from the previous two quizzes, and also includes a composition. Your students should practice writing this paragraph before taking the final.

Reading Notes

Stillwater   the pleasant little city in which the Poppers live

calcimine   whitewash

daresay   expression that means "think it likely"

litter   objects thrown about

Vocabulary

1. he was rather an **untidy** man _____

   _____

2. Mr. Popper was so **absent-minded** … always dreaming about far-away countries _____

   _____

3. That was what he **regretted** most of all. _____

   _____

4. He had never seen those great shining white **expanses** of ice and snow

   _____

5. he might have joined some of the great Polar **expeditions** _____

   _____

6. When he came to the gate of the neat little **bungalow** _____

   _____

Comprehension Questions

1. What is Mr. Popper's occupation? _____

   _____

   _____

2. What does Mr. Popper dream about most? What far-away places does Mr. Popper wish to see most of all?

   _____

   _____

   _____

3. Why are evenings the best time of all for Mr Popper? _____

_____

_____

4. Why is Mr. Popper happy it is the end of September? _____

_____

_____

5. What is Mrs. Popper worried about? How will the family manage during the winter months? _____

_____

_____

_____

_____

Quotations

No one knew what went on inside of Mr. Popper's head, and no one guessed that he would one day be the most famous person in Stillwater.

Discussion Questions

1. What is one word that adequately sums up Mr. Popper's character?
2. Although Mr. Popper cannot join a Polar expedition, how does he compensate for this?

Enrichment

1. Draw a picture of the Popper family. Use details from the book.
2. Find the locations Mr. Popper dreamed about on a map. Guess why each might appeal to him.
3. Think of an exotic place you would like to visit. Explain your choice.
4. Write five sentences that describe Mr. Popper and his family. Use details from the book and choose your own strong adjectives.

Reading Notes

spectacles	eyeglasses
Ladies' Aid and Missionary Society	an organization formed by the women in a town or church
broadcasting	the sending of messages through electronic means, such as radio

Vocabulary

1. answered Mrs. Popper, a little **sharply** _____

   _____

2. She was not at all a disagreeable woman, but she sometimes got rather **cross**

   _____

3. They walk **erect** like little men _____

   _____

4. They sound to me like pretty **heathen** birds. _____

   _____

5. It's a **queer** thing. _____

   _____

6. Mr. Popper put down his book … and moved **hastily** to the radio. _____

   _____

7. from the South Pole, a **faint** voice floated out into the Popper living room _____

   _____

Comprehension Questions

1. What impresses Mr. Popper most about the Drake Expedition?_____

   _____

   _____

2. What words does Mr. Popper use to describe penguins to Mrs. Popper?_____

   _____

   _____

3. How are penguins different from other birds? _____

_____

_____

_____

_____

4. Why is Mr. Popper excited about September 29th? _____

_____

_____

5. What unexpected event happens that day? _____

_____

_____

6. What does Admiral Drake tell Mr. Popper to watch for? _____

_____

_____

_____

Quotations

"Hello, Mr. Popper, up there in Stillwater. Thanks for your nice letter about the pictures of our last expedition. Watch for an answer. But not by letter, Mr. Popper. Watch for a surprise. Signing off. Signing off."

Who said this? _____   From where? _____

Discussion Questions

1. In Chapter 1, Mr. Popper was described as a dreamer. How would you describe Mrs. Popper in contrast to her husband?

Enrichment

1. Find an old *National Geographic* magazine and read about exotic places.

2. Make a picture collage of exotic places you would like to visit. Locate them on a map or globe.

3. Learn about the differences between the North and South Poles.

4. Research the Poles and penguins. Write a paragraph detailing a penguin's natural habitat and daily routines.

Reading Notes

receipt   a paper that lists the money or goods you have received

debris   waste

Captain Cook   a famous explorer in the 18th century from England

Vocabulary

1. "Very well, my love," said Mr. Popper **meekly** _____
   _____

2. It was an **expressman** with the largest box Mr. Popper had ever seen. _____
   _____

3. part of the packing, which was a layer of **dry ice** _____
   _____

4. His hands were trembling so that he could **scarcely** lift off the last of the wrappings.
   _____

5. Down the hall it went and into the bedrooms, with its strange, **pompous** little strut.
   _____

6. the **inquisitive** bird kept reaching over and trying to bite the faucets _____
   _____

7. with outstretched flippers, **tobogganed** down on its white stomach _____
   _____

Comprehension Questions

1. Describe the package that is delivered to Mr. Popper. _____
   _____
   _____

2. What emerges from the box? _____
   _____
   _____

3. Describe the gift in detail. _____

_____

_____

4. Why is the bathroom so attractive to the guest? _____

_____

_____

5. Why does Mr. Popper fill the bathtub?_____

_____

_____

6. How does the guest get his name? _____

_____

_____

Quotations

It was a stout little fellow about two and a half feet high. Although it was about the size of a small child, it looked much more like a little gentleman, with its smooth white waistcoat in front and its long black tailcoat dragging a little behind. Its eyes were set in two white circles in its black head. It turned its head from one side to the other, as first with one eye and then with the other, it examined Mr. Popper.

Whom is this describing? _____

Discussion Questions

1. Why does Mr. Popper have a difficult time sleeping that night?

2. When morning comes, why is Mr. Popper sorry that he has nowhere to go and nothing to do?

3. Describe Mr. Popper's reaction as he opens the package and discovers the penguin.

Enrichment

1. Research the historical significance of the name Captain Cook.

2. Track the real Captain Cook's route on a map or globe.

3. Write a vivid description of the package that Mr. Popper received. Be sure to appeal to each of the five senses. Consider how you want your reader to respond to your description. Do you want him to be scared of the box? Excited about the box? Curious about it? Try to appeal to your reader's emotion when describing the package.

Reading Notes

English   someone from Great Britain

American Revolution   the war in which the American colonists won their independence from Britain

washstand   a stand holding a basin and pitcher for washing one's hands

upholstered   having a cover or cushion (furniture)

Vocabulary

1. I think Captain Cook would be a very **suitable** name _____

_____

2. suddenly getting **lively** again_____

_____

3. "Stop him, Papa!" screamed Mrs. Popper, **retreating** into the hallway _____

_____

4. "Gork?" he inquired … looking at her **pleadingly** with his right eye. _____

_____

5. Then he walked **solemnly** around the table … inspecting everything. _____

_____

6. Then he left the door **ajar** so that the penguin would have plenty of fresh air

_____

Comprehension Questions

1. Why does Mr. Popper name his penguin Captain Cook? _____

_____

_____

2. How does Captain Cook get in trouble with Mrs. Popper? _____

_____

_____

3. Describe Captain Cook's sleeping quarters. _____

_____

_____

4. Why does Mrs. Popper believe the penguin will be a good example for the children? _____

_____

_____

5. List several things Mr. Popper does to make Captain Cook more comfortable in his new home. _____

_____

_____

_____

Quotations

"Well, dear me, I never thought we would have a penguin for a pet. Still, he behaves pretty well, on the whole, and he is so nice and clean that perhaps he will be a good example to you and the children."

Who said this? _____

Discussion Questions

1. Why does Mr. Popper think Captain Cook is a suitable name for a penguin?
2. How do the Poppers realize that Captain Cook (the penguin) knows he has done wrong after eating the goldfish?

Enrichment

1. Research the American Revolution.
2. Read about training penguins.
3. Draw a picture of Captain Cook in his new home.

Reading Notes

service man   a person who repairs appliances and equipment

icebox   refrigerator

license   a certificate granting permission from the government to do something

Vocabulary

1. Mister, you don't need no **ventilating** holes in that there door. _____
   _____

2. He didn't want to discuss Captain Cook with this **unsympathetic** service man _____
   _____

3. "Don't get funny," said Mr. Popper **indignantly**. _____
   _____

4. the service man had no **intention** of putting on an inside handle _____
   _____

5. That's the first **sensible** thing you've said yet. _____
   _____

6. Mr. Popper **promptly** put Captain Cook back inside _____
   _____

Comprehension Questions

1. The first sentence on page 31 says, "The next day was quite eventful." Explain why. _____
   _____
   _____
   _____

2. Why does the service man think Mr. Popper is "not quite right"? _____
   _____
   _____

3. How does Mr. Popper finally get the service man to put a handle on the inside of the door? _____
   _____

4. What does Captain Cook think of his new entrance to his quarters? _____

_____

_____

5. Why do you think the policeman visits the Popper home? _____

_____

_____

Quotations

The next day was quite eventful at 432 Proudfoot Avenue. First there was the service man and then the policeman and then the trouble about the license.

Discussion Questions

1. After the service man and Mr. Popper begin arguing, why does Mr. Popper not just simply explain to the service man that he is going to keep a penguin in the refrigerator? Do you think it would have helped if he had?

2. How much money did Mr. Popper give to the service man in total? Why? How did he feel about giving away the money?

3. What is one character quality used to describe Captain Cook several times in this chapter as well as in previous chapters? How does this quality get him into trouble, and how does it help him adjust to new situations?

Enrichment

1. Think of other places in a home or neighborhood that a penguin might like to live.

2. Write a list of other types of homes for a penguin. Rank them from most desirable to least desirable for a penguin.

3. Re-tell the exciting events of the day in a five-sentence paragraph. Start by writing five sentences, using the cue words **first**, **second**, **third**, **next**, and **finally** to start your sentences. Improve each sentence and then combine them to form a paragraph. Be sure to indent the first sentence of your paragraph and punctuate every sentence correctly.

Reading Notes

municipal ordinance	city law
sergeant	an officer in the police force
Bureau	governmental agency

Vocabulary

1. "Gook," said Captain Cook walking with **dignity** _____

_____

2. the penguin did his best to **disconnect** the telephone by biting the green cord _____

_____

3. This went on for **considerable** time. _____

_____

4. And please try to speak a little more **distinctly** _____

_____

5. "Then listen," roared Mr. Popper, now completely **outraged**. _____

_____

Comprehension Questions

1. Why doesn't the policeman come inside the Poppers' house? _____

_____

_____

2. How does the conversation with the policeman end? _____

_____

_____

3. What does Captain Cook do to make the phone call more difficult for Mr. Popper?

_____

_____

4. Describe two people Mr. Popper talks to before he finally hangs up the telephone.

_____

_____

5. Does Mr. Popper resolve his problem with the people at City Hall? _____

_____

_____

Quotations

Even so, he found it was not so easy to learn whether or not he must get a license for his strange pet. Every time he would explain what he wanted, he would be told to wait a minute, and much later a new voice would ask him what he wanted. This went on for considerable time.

Discussion Questions

1. Why do you think that the service man and the policeman seem so unfamiliar with penguins?
2. Why do you think Mr. Popper hangs up the telephone without acquiring a license for Captain Cook?

Enrichment

1. Look up the ordinances for the place where you live. Note any interesting rules.
2. Are there any rules related to animals for your neighborhood, town, city, or county?
3. Write a paragraph to summarize Mr. Popper's phone call to City Hall. Use interesting details about each person Mr. Popper spoke with, and explain the result of each conversation. Be sure to include Mr. Popper's reactions.

Reading Notes

market	where shopping is done
housekeeper	one who manages and cleans the home
Parcheesi cup	used for rolling the dice in the game of Parcheesi
rookery	a collection of nests for birds such as penguins

Vocabulary

1. Very **reluctantly**, Janie and Bill had to leave Captain Cook and go to school.

    _____

2. Mrs. Popper was busy in the kitchen, rather **belatedly** doing the breakfast dishes

    _____

3. she **dimly** realized that the penguin was going in and out the refrigerator pretty frequently _____

    _____

4. Meanwhile Mr. Popper had **abandoned** his telephoning and was now busy shaving

    _____

5. But the penguin … was by no means **idle**. _____

    _____

6. with little **subdued** cries of curiosity, surprise, and pleasure _____

    _____

7. Never again would Mrs. Popper have to **reproach** him for looking as wild as a lion.

    _____

Comprehension Questions

1. Why has Mr. Popper made himself neat? _____

    _____

    _____

2. What is Captain Cook working on during the morning chores? _____

    _____

    _____

3. List some of the most interesting items in Captain Cook's nest. _____

_____

_____

4. What does Mr. Popper call Captain Cook's nest? _____

_____

5. Describe how Mr. Popper looks when he takes Captain Cook out for a walk.

_____

_____

_____

6. Find out what these words and phrases mean:

flannel trousers _____

oxblood shoes _____

cedar chest _____

tailcoat _____

Quotations

And each time he found what he seemed to be looking for, he picked it up in the black end of his red beak, and carried it, waddling proudly on his wide, pink feet, into the kitchen, and into the icebox.

Discussion Questions

1. Why does Mrs. Popper think Captain Cook is going to be a help around the house?
2. Why do you think Mr. Popper wants the clothesline from Mamma?

Enrichment

1. Write a list of every item Captain Cook included in his nest. How many items were there all together?
2. Draw a picture of Captain Cook's nest.
3. Research rookeries. Find out how penguins usually build them. List interesting facts about rookeries and penguins' nests on another piece of paper. Include the facts in a report.
4. **Alliteration** is when the beginning consonant sound of two or more words in a sentence is the same. Authors use alliteration to make their story more memorable and give their writing a poetic quality. Here is an example of alliteration from *Mr. Popper's Penguins*:

   "Into the corners of every room he prowled and poked and pecked."

   See if you can find other examples from the book.

Reading Notes

derby	a type of hat
dodo	a large, clumsy, flightless bird, now extinct
tripod	a three-legged stand

Vocabulary

1. when he saw that protesting did him no good, he recovered his **customary** dignity

   _____

2. Heaven **preserve** us! _____

   _____

3. These he **evidently** mistook for polar snow _____

   _____

4. for he began to peck at the window **vigorously** _____

   _____

5. Captain Cook, however, was still too much interested in the window **exhibits** to bother to turn around.

   _____

6. I'd think it was a dodo, only dodos are **extinct**. _____

   _____

7. At last, Captain Cook, standing still beside Mr. Popper, **consented** to pose.

   _____

Comprehension Questions

1. What did Captain Cook think of the leash? _____

   _____

   _____

   _____

2. Describe how Mr. Popper conducts his walk with Captain Cook. _____

   _____

   _____

3. How does Mrs. Callahan react to seeing the penguins? _____

_____

_____

4. How had the two young men from the newspaper learned of the strange bird? _____

_____

_____

5. What two kinds of birds do the photographer and the cameraman guess Captain Cook might be? _____

_____

_____

6. How did they convince themselves otherwise? _____

_____

_____

Quotations

Mr. Popper put on his best Sunday derby and opened the front door with Captain Cook waddling graciously beside him.

"Gook!" said Captain Cook, and raising his flippers, he leaned forward bravely and tobogganed down the steps on his stomach.

Discussion Questions

1. Reread the last quotation above. Why do you think the author describes Captain Cook's actions as brave?
2. Why do you think the reporter does not believe Mr. Popper when he explains how Captain Cook came to live with him?

Enrichment

1. Research pelicans and dodos.
2. Compare and contrast penguins, pelicans, and dodos.
3. Draw a picture of each bird.
4. Write a paragraph on dodos or pelicans. Read it aloud to the class.

Illustrating a Scene

In the box below, choose and illustrate a scene from what you have read so far.
Use visual details so that anyone who looks at your drawing will be able to recognize
the characters, setting, and action.

Illustrating a Scene

In the box below, choose and illustrate a scene from what you have read so far.
Use visual details so that anyone who looks at your drawing will be able to recognize
the characters, setting, and action.

Reading Notes

barbershop	a shop where men have their hair cut and get a shave
ledge	a narrow projection protruding from a wall or other surface
lather	the foam produced when soap is mixed with water
alley	a narrow lane running between buildings or at the back of a street

Vocabulary

1. Captain Cook found this **spectacle** very interesting _____
   _____

2. Mr. Popper took Captain Cook in his arms, and **amid** cries … made his way out of the shop _____
   _____

3. "All right," said Mr. Popper, **panting** up the steps behind Captain Cook.
   _____

4. Slowly but **unwearyingly**, Captain Cook lifted one pink foot after another from one step to the next ____
   _____

5. Mr. Popper had to call a taxi to **distract** him.
   _____

6. The driver … did not laugh at his **oddly assorted** passengers until he had been paid.
   _____

7. he went to lie down, for he was quite **exhausted** from all the unusual exercise
   _____

Comprehension Questions

1. Why does the barber order Captain Cook out of his shop?_____
   _____
   _____

2. What is "absolutely impossible" to keep Captain Cook from doing? _____
   _____
   _____

3. What does Mr. Popper conclude is the reason Captain Cook loves the activity?

_____

_____

4. How does the taxi driver respond to Mr. Popper and his penguin? _____

_____

_____

_____

5. Describe how Mr. Popper feels at the end of his walk with Captain Cook.

_____

_____

Quotations

"Oh dear!" said Mrs. Popper, when she opened the door to her husband. "You looked so neat and handsome when you started for your walk. And now look at the front of you!"

"I am sorry, my love," said Mr. Popper in a humble tone, "but you can't always tell what a penguin will do next."

Discussion Questions

1. Why does tying one end of the clothesline to his wrist prove unwise for Mr. Popper?
2. Reread the second quote. What is a character trait you have noticed about Mr. Popper? When are some other times throughout the story you have noticed this?

Enrichment

1. Have a class discussion about animals that live with your family.
2. If you don't have any pets, imagine what kind of pet you would like to have.
3. Draw a picture of your real or imaginary pet. Write its name on the picture.
4. Write a letter to Mr. Popper offering new suggestions on how he might take Captain Cook on a walk. Explain why you think your method will work.

Reading Notes

chronicle   a newspaper

rotogravure   the photography section of a newspaper

sherbet   a frozen treat made with fruit and fruit juices served between courses or as a dessert

curator   the director of a museum or the guardian of a museum's collections

Vocabulary

1. He had suddenly **ceased** his gay, exploring little walks about the house

    _____

2. He had suddenly ceased his **gay**, exploring little walks about the house

    _____

3. would sit most of the day, **sulking**, in the refrigerator   _____

    _____

4. it was something worse than mopiness that **ailed** Captain Cook _____

    _____

5. I think you had better call the **veterinary doctor**.   _____

    _____

6. an Antarctic penguin can't **thrive** in Stillwater   _____

    _____

7. He slept all day now in a heavy **stupor**   _____

    _____

Comprehension Questions

1. How do the Poppers know something is wrong with Captain Cook?_____

    _____

    _____

    _____

2. What does the doctor prescribe for the sick penguin? _____

    _____

    _____

3. Why does he think the case is hopeless? _____

_____

_____

4. As a last resort, what does Mr. Popper do to help Captain Cook? _____

_____

_____

5. What is the grand result of Mr. Popper's effort? _____

_____

_____

Quotations

All the Poppers had grown terribly fond of the funny, solemn little chap, and Mr. Popper's heart was frozen with terror. It seemed to him that his life would be very empty if Captain Cook went away.

Discussion Questions

1. How does everyone show their sympathy for Captain Cook when he is sick? Does anything help?
2. How do the Poppers feel when they think that Captain Cook is going to die?
3. What does Dr. Smith think ails both Captain Cook and Greta, the penguin at the aquarium?
4. Why do you think this chapter is titled "Shadows"?

Enrichment

1. Find out if there are penguins at the zoo in your city. Visit them if you are able.
2. Write a letter to a veterinarian or a zoo to inquire about the penguins there. Ask the zookeeper to share any information available on how to care for a penguin. Share with your class any response you receive.

Reading Notes

cellar   a basement or rooms below the house

overcoat   a long, heavy coat for use in winter

blizzard   a storm of snow and gusty winds

Vocabulary

1. he's trying to show that he's **grateful** to us for getting him Greta _____ _____

2. **squirming** around in her nest, she turned her back to Mr. Popper _____ _____

3. there were large **drifts** of snow all over the house _____ _____

4. Both Greta and Captain Cook were **tremendously** pleased with all that ice. _____

5. But Captain Cook and Greta are both fat and **sleek**. _____ _____

6. the children have never been so **rosy** _____ _____

Comprehension Questions

1. What does Captain Cook do to show his appreciation to Mr. Popper?

   _____

   _____

2. How do the Poppers mark Captain Cook and Greta to tell them apart?

   _____

   _____

3. What worries Mrs. Popper about Captain Cook's and Greta's living space?

   _____

   _____

4. List some things the Poppers do to accommodate the penguins.

_____

_____

_____

5. Describe how the floor is made into an ice rink. _____ _____

_____

_____

Quotations

Both Greta and Captain Cook were tremendously pleased with all that ice. They would go up on the snowdrift at one end of the living room, and run down, one behind the other, onto the ice, until they were running too fast to keep their balance. Then they would flop on their stomachs and and toboggan across the slippery ice.

Discussion Questions

1. How does a penguin at the South Pole show its friendship?

2. Why does Mrs. Popper demand that Mr. Popper do something when the ice in their living room begins to melt? How does Mr. Popper feel?

Enrichment

1. What other methods could you use to identify the penguins in a helpful, yet unharmful way?

2. Draw a picture of the Poppers' house with the blizzard inside.

3. Write a paragraph describing the Poppers' house with the blizzard inside. Detail the way the house looked and how the Poppers reacted to the wintery weather. Use strong adjectives and clear descriptions. Include adverbs to make your verbs more interesting.

Reading Notes

engineer	design specialist or technologist
credit	a loan
marching drills	parades

Vocabulary

1. a large freezing plant **installed** in the cellar

   _____

2. Mr. Popper was quite worried when he found that all these changes were going to be very **expensive**.

   _____

3. They were fuzzy, **droll** little creatures who grew at a tremendous rate. _____

   _____

4. two of them ... began to **spar** at each other with their flippers _____

   _____

5. Louisa seemed especially **fond** _____

   _____

6. he **dreaded** to think of the time when spring would come _____

   _____

Comprehension Questions

1. What does the engineer install in the Poppers' cellar? What happens to their furnace? _____

   _____

   _____

   _____

2. How many eggs do penguins usually lay per season? How many eggs does Greta lay in total, and how

   frequently does an egg appear? _____

   _____

   _____

   _____

3. What problem do the eggs create? _____

_____

_____

4. How does Mr. Popper resolve the problem? _____

_____

_____

5. Name the penguin children. _____

_____

_____

_____

6. Describe the eating habits of the penguins. _____

_____

_____

_____

Quotations

Since Mr. Popper knew that penguins lay only two eggs a season, he was astonished when, a little later, the third egg was found under Greta. Whether the change in climate had changed the penguins' breeding habits, Mr. Popper never knew, but every third day a new one would appear until there were ten in all.

Discussion Questions

1. Why is Mr. Popper worried after he has the engineer install a large freezing plant in the cellar? Why is the engineer worried? What arrangement do they come to?

2. Describe the freezing plant in the cellar and explain why it is a good one. What else does Mr. Popper do to his cellar for the penguins?

3. How does Mr. Popper now spend his evenings? What does he think about?

Enrichment

1. List each of the children's names. Try to discover why Mr. Popper chose each name. Remember Mr. Popper's interests and hobbies.

2. Write a sentence explaining the historical significance of each of the young penguins' names.

Reading Notes

costumes   clothes worn by a performer

theater   the building in which a play or performance takes place

Vocabulary

1. It's been easier than usual to keep the place **tidy** _____

_____

2. Well, I don't **suppose** I really could enjoy eating them. _____

_____

3. you have heard of **trained** seals, acting in theaters _____

_____

4. Janie and Bill would drag out into the middle of the ice two **portable** stepladders

_____

5. Mrs. Popper would play a pretty, **descriptive** piece called "By the Brook." _____

_____

Comprehension Questions

1. What new worry does Mrs. Popper have?_____

_____

_____

2. What suggestions does Mrs. Popper have for fixing the problem? _____

_____

_____

3. What is Mr. Popper's suggestion? _____

_____

_____

4. What do the Poppers do to implement Mr. Popper's plan? _____

_____

_____

5. Describe the penguins' acts. _____

_____

_____

_____

Quotations

"What these penguins like to do most is to drill like an army, to watch Nelson and Columbus get in a fight with each other, and to climb up steps and toboggan down. And so we will build our act around those tricks."

Who said this? _____

Discussion Questions

1. How does Mrs. Popper help Mr. Popper implement his plan to train the penguins? How do June and Bill help?

Enrichment

1. Listen to Schubert's "Military March" and Franz Lehár's "Merry Widow Waltz," and describe the songs using strong adjectives. Do you think these were good musical selections for the acts the penguins performed?

2. Learn about Schubert, the composer of the "Military March."

3. Write a detailed description of your favorite trick that the penguins performed. Explain it clearly for someone who has not read this book.

Reading Notes

fare   the cost to travel on public transportation

transfers   free tokens for changing bus lines

chorus girls   theatrical dancers

Vocabulary

1. before the astonished driver could **protest**, they had all climbed on and the bus was on its way. _____
_____

2. I'm just taking them down to the Palace to **interview** Mr. Greenbaum _____
_____

3. It took Mr. Popper quite a while to open the windows, which were stuck **fast**.
_____

4. "Hello," said the theater manager, as the Poppers and the penguins **trooped** past him.
_____

5. Their twenty-four white-circled eyes were very **solemn** _____
_____

6. This is a private **conference**. _____
_____

Comprehension Questions

1. Describe the Poppers' trip to the theater. _____
_____
_____

2. Why does the family get kicked off the bus? _____
_____
_____

3. What name does Mr. Popper want to call the group of penguins? _____
_____
_____

4. What name does Mr. Greenbaum suggest for the group? _____

_____

_____

5. Why does Mr. Popper decline? _____

_____

_____

Quotations

That evening—it was Saturday, the twenty-ninth of January—the Popper family and their twelve trained penguins, two of them carrying flags in their beaks, left the house to find the Palace Theater.

Discussion Questions

1. Whom does Mr. Popper discover is in town, and why do they go to see him?

2. Give several examples from this chapter of how well-trained and well-behaved the penguins are.

Enrichment

1. Draw a picture of the penguins walking to the bus stop. Label each person or penguin.

2. Draw a poster advertising Popper's Performing Penguins.

3. Write an advertisement for Popper's Performing Penguins. Explain why someone would want to see the penguins' performance, using carefully chosen words. Remember, in an advertisement you have a very limited opportunity to make your point—every word must be well chosen!

Studying Characters

Write the name of each listed character on the line above that character's description.
Each name can be used only one time.

Characters	Descriptions

Characters

Mr. Popper

Mrs. Popper

Janie

Captain Cook

Mr. Greenbaum

Admiral Drake

Greta

Bill

Descriptions

_____
saved Captain Cook

_____
dreams about far-away places

_____
the first penguin

_____
owns many theaters

_____
the Poppers' son

_____
worries about money in winter

_____
South Pole explorer

_____
the Poppers' daughter

Illustrating a Scene

In the box below, choose and illustrate a scene from what you have read so far.
Use visual details so that anyone who looks at your drawing will be able to recognize
the characters, setting, and action.

Reading Notes

manager   the person in charge of a business or performance

stage   a platform that has been raised for actors to perform on

semicircle   half a circle

Vocabulary

1. with your kind **indulgence** we are going to try out a little **novelty** number tonight.

    a)_____ b) _____

2. Owing to **unforeseen circumstances**, the Marvelous Marcos are unable to appear

    _____

3. In a **dignified** way the Poppers and the penguins walked out on the stage

    _____

4. wheeling and changing their **formations** with great **precision**

    a)_____ b) _____

5. Columbus then counted ten over the **prostrate** Nelson _____

    _____

6. you've got something absolutely **unique** in those birds. Your act is a **sensation**.

    a)_____ b) _____

7. the way you helped out my friend … shows that you're real **troupers** _____

    _____

Comprehension Questions

1. How do the penguins get the chance to perform for a live audience?_____

    _____

    _____

2. Describe the audience's reaction to the first act._____

    _____

    _____

3. What does Mr. Greenbaum think of the performance? What does Mr. Greenbaum predict? _____

_____

_____

_____

4. Detail the offer that is made to the Poppers. How do the Poppers feel about the deal? _____

_____

_____

_____

5. What lesson does the manager want the penguins to teach the ushers?

_____

_____

Quotations

"I don't mind telling you, Mr. Popper, that I think you've got something absolutely unique in those birds. Your act is a sensation. And the way you helped out my friend the manager, here, shows that you're real troupers—the kind we need in the show business."

Who said this? _____

Discussion Questions

1. Describe the sparring contest between Nelson and Columbus. Who wins and why?

Enrichment

1. List the ten stops in the U.S. you would make if you were able to map the penguins' tours.
2. On a U.S. map, plot your "wish trip" in the most efficient way, marking the stops in the order you would make them (Stop #1, 2, 3, etc.).
3. Explain your reasons for choosing the ten stops you would make on the penguins' tour.

Reading Notes

sixes and sevens	in disarray
moth balls	small balls containing chemicals used to ward off moths
clergyman's collar	white band under a black shirt collar, as a priest would wear
baggage	luggage
berths	bunk beds

Vocabulary

1. Mr. Greenbaum sent them their first week's pay in **advance**. _____ _____

2. The porter's ladders offered too much **temptation** to the penguins. _____

3. There were a dozen happy Orks from a dozen **ecstatic** beaks. _____ _____

4. you must remember, my love, that travel is very **broadening**. _____ _____

5. From the start the penguins were a **riotous** success. _____ _____

6. It was here that the penguins added a little **novelty** number of their own to the program. _____ _____

Comprehension Questions

1. What do the Poppers do with their first week's advance pay? _____ _____ _____

2. What happens on the way to the station? How are the Poppers partly responsible? _____ _____ _____

3. How do the penguins misbehave on the train? _____

_____

_____

4. How do audiences respond to the penguins' performances? _____

_____

_____

_____

5. Describe the scene with the penguins and the tightrope walker, Monsieur Duval.

_____

_____

_____

Quotations

From the start the penguins were a riotous success.

And whenever they appeared, the more they interfered with the other acts on the program the better the audiences liked them.

To whom does this refer? _____

Discussion Questions

1. Compare the different ways that Mr. and Mrs. Popper feel about their children missing school initially. Whom do you agree with, and why?

Enrichment

1. Read about trains. What were they like for travel? What were popular train routes in the U.S.? What happened to the railroad lines?

2. Why do most people not travel by train anymore? Have you ever taken a trip on a passenger train?

3. When did this story take place? Write at least five sentences describing the clues that let you know the story did not take place in the present time and that might support your guess.

Reading Notes

testimonial   statement of truth

orchestra pit   where the orchestra plays at a theater, usually in front of the stage but on a lower level than the audience

bell boy   a porter at a hotel who carries luggage and delivers messages for customers

contract   a written agreement

Vocabulary

1. a celebrated lady opera singer got very much **annoyed**

    _____

2. in another minute the audience was **shrieking** with laughter

    _____

3. That stopped the singing entirely except for one high, **shrill** note

    _____

4. Now and then a **startled** hotelkeeper would object to having the birds

    _____

5. Mr. Popper, who never liked to be a **nuisance** to anyone, always took taxis

    _____

6. Wherever they went, their **reputation** traveled ahead of them.

    _____

Comprehension Questions

1. Why did other performers not like to be scheduled with the penguins? _____

    _____

    _____

2. What do the penguins do to disrupt the opera singer's performance? _____

    _____

    _____

3. What do the penguins think about performing and traveling? _____

_____

_____

4. How do the penguins behave at hotels? What are their worst misbehaviors? _____

_____

_____

_____

_____

5. How do the Poppers earn extra income? _____

_____

_____

Quotations

The birds soon became so famous that whenever it was known that the Popper Performing Penguins were to appear at any theater, the crowds would stand in line for half a mile down the street, waiting their turn to buy tickets.

Discussion Questions

1. Are the Poppers making money from their show? Why or why not?
2. Why would the hotelkeepers eventually allow the penguins to stay at their hotels even though they were concerned at first?
3. Why does Mr. Popper refuse to recommend the products of the spinach and oat companies? What does this say about his character?

Enrichment

1. List the cities the Poppers will visit on their tour. Spell each correctly and name the state it is in.
2. Map the Poppers' course on a map. Compare it to your "wish trip."
3. What do you know about each city they will visit?
4. Think of a product that you really like or appreciate. Write a testimonial for it, trying to persuade others to use it or buy it.

Reading Notes

insured	having financial coverage in the event of any loss or damage
patrol	guards for keeping order
warrant	court order

Vocabulary

1. "Yes sir," said the driver, **threading** his way in and out the traffic

   _____

2. In the wings stood a large **burly**, red-faced man.

   _____

3. From the stage could be heard the **hoarse** barks of the seals

   _____

4. the audience was in an **uproar**, and the curtain was quickly rung down.

   _____

5. they were a little **vexed** to find that there was no fire at all

   _____

6. You're a **disturber** of the peace.

   _____

Comprehension Questions

1. What does Mr. Popper think about when he sees the penguins on the roof?

   _____

   _____

2. Who else is performing at the Regal Theater? Why is this a potential problem?

   _____

   _____

3. How do the policemen and the firemen get involved in the action? What are the teams?

   _____

   _____

4. What do the Poppers find when they go to check on the penguins and the seals?

_____

_____

5. What action does the theater manager take against Mr. Popper? _____

_____

_____

Quotations

"You've broken into my theater and thrown the place into a panic, that's what you've done. You're a disturber of the peace."

Who said this? _____   About whom? _____

Discussion Questions

1. Describe the unusual weather taking place this spring. How does it affect the penguins?
2. What causes Mr. Popper to make his great mistake of asking the taxi driver to take him to the wrong theater?

Enrichment

1. Why do you think seals are often used in circus acts?
2. Draw a picture of the conflict between the seals and the penguins.
3. Research seals. Write a paragraph describing their habitat and daily activities. Read your paragraph to your class.

Reading Notes

bail	money used to release prisoners from jail
Hollywood	the city in California where many films are directed and produced
corridor	hallway

Vocabulary

1. None of his **pleas** could move the desk sergeant.

   _____

2. I'm going to give you all a nice quiet cell—unless you **furnish** bail.

   _____

3. Even the younger birds sat all day in **dismal** silence

   _____

4. Mr. Greenbaum would probably turn up … to see about **renewing** the contract.

   _____

5. Then, as his eyes became **accustomed** to the light, he looked again.

   _____

6. Here's Mr. Klein, who owns the **Colossal** Film Company.

   _____

7. said the admiral **judiciously** _____

   _____

Comprehension Questions

1. How much bail money has to be paid for their release? Why can't Mr. Popper pay the bail?

   _____

   _____

   _____

2. Why do the penguins begin to droop in jail? _____

   _____

   _____

   _____

3. Whom does Mr. Popper expect to bail him out of jail? Who comes to see Mr. Popper instead?

_____

_____

4. What does Admiral Drake offer Mr. Popper? _____

_____

_____

_____

5. What does Mr. Klein offer Mr. Popper? _____

_____

_____

Quotations

It was not Mr. Greenbaum who stood there. It was a great, bearded man in a splendid uniform. Smiling, he held out his hand to Mr. Popper.

Who is the surprise visitor instead of Mr. Greenbaum? _____

Discussion Questions

1. Why does Admiral Drake want to establish a breed of penguins at the North Pole?

2. How does Mrs. Popper feel about Mr. Klein's offer? What does Mr. Popper say about his two very different offers? What do you think would be the best decision, and why?

Enrichment

1. To compare two things means to find their similarities. To contrast means to find the differences. Write a paragraph that compares two things and contrasts two things about the North and South Poles.

Reading Notes

advantages   benefits

quarters   lodgings

vessels   boats or ships

gangplank   a board used for walking on or off a ship

anchor   the heavy hook that holds a ship in place while it is still in the water

Vocabulary

1. she pointed these out, without trying to **influence** him _____

_____

2. It was a pale and **haggard** Mr. Popper who was ready to announce his decision

_____

3. Every day huge boxes of supplies of all sorts were **hustled** on board._____

_____

4. the extraordinary penguins that were a real **contribution** to science.

_____

5. **scuttled** up on deck _____

_____

Comprehension Questions

1. Which offer does Mr. Popper decide to accept? _____

_____

_____

2. What does Mr. Popper agree to let Mr. Klein do? How much does he pay him? _____

_____

_____

_____

3. What preparations are made for the voyage? _____

_____

_____

4. How do the penguins react to the boat? _____

_____

_____

5. What exciting surprise does Mr. Popper receive as the boat is about to set sail? _____

_____

_____

Quotations

"Man alive, aren't those penguins the reason for this whole Expedition? And who's going to see that they're well and happy if you're not along? Go put on one of those fur suits, like the rest of us. We're pulling anchor in a minute."

Who said this? _____   To whom? _____

Discussion Questions

1. What are Mr. Popper's reasons for deciding to give the penguins to Admiral Drake?
2. What keeps Mr. Popper's heart from breaking as he says goodbye to his penguins? What does this say about his character?

Enrichment

1. Draw a picture of Mr. Popper departing for the Expedition with Admiral Drake.

Illustrating a Scene

In the box below, choose and illustrate a scene from *Mr. Popper's Penguins*.
Use visual details so that anyone who looks at your drawing will be able to recognize the characters, setting, and action.